Innerkip, Ontario including Woodstock and Area in Photos, Saving Our History One Photo at a Time

Photography
by Barbara Raué
2012

Series Name:
Cruising Ontario

Book 17: Innerkip

Cover photo: 134 Blandford Street, Innerkip

Series Name: Cruising Ontario

Book 1: London
Book 2: Dundas
Book 3: Hamilton
Book 4: Oakville
Book 5: Chesley
Book 6: Stoney Creek
Book 7: Waterdown
Book 8: Owen Sound
Book 9: Mount Forest
Book 10: Dundalk
Book 11: Burford and Area
Book 12: Waterford and Area
Book 13: Drumbo and Area
Book 14: Sheffield and Area
Book 15: Tavistock and Area
Book 16: Ancaster
Book 17: Innerkip, Woodstock and Area

Other Books by Barbara Raue

Coins and Gems

Arrows, Indians and Love

The Life and Times of Barbara
Volume 1: Inventions That Have Enhanced My Life
Volume 2: Entertainment That I Have Enjoyed
Volume 3: East Coast Trip 2009
Volume 4: Olympics
Volume 5: Wonders of the World

Innerkip

Innerkip is located on Oxford Road 29 north of Highway 401, northeast of Woodstock.

Woodstock

Woodstock is located along the Thames River at the junction of Highways 401 and 403, west of Brantford, east of London. The community was first settled in 1800 by American immigrants from New York state. Settlers from Great Britain arrived in the 1820s and 1830s.

Huntingford

Huntingford is located on County Road 59, north of Woodstock, west of Innerkip.

Punkeydoodles Corners

Punkeydoodles Corners is located four miles east of Tavistock. Today the corner has a scattering of houses and farms. At one time it was a bustling stop along the Huron Road. The most popular legend about how it got its name is from the song "Yankee Doodle Dandy" which was popular in the 1800s and often sung around the piano at the inn and tavern located at the Corner during the late nineteenth century. Today, the corner is the meeting place of three districts – Oxford County, Perth County and the Region of Waterloo.

Hickson

Hickson is located on Oxford County Road 8 (Loveys Street), north of Woodstock, southwest of New Hamburg.

Innerkip

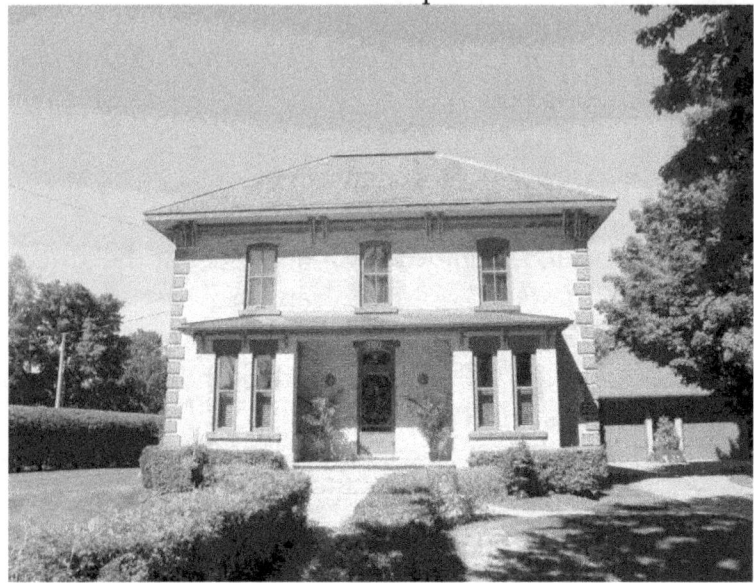

190 Blandford Street

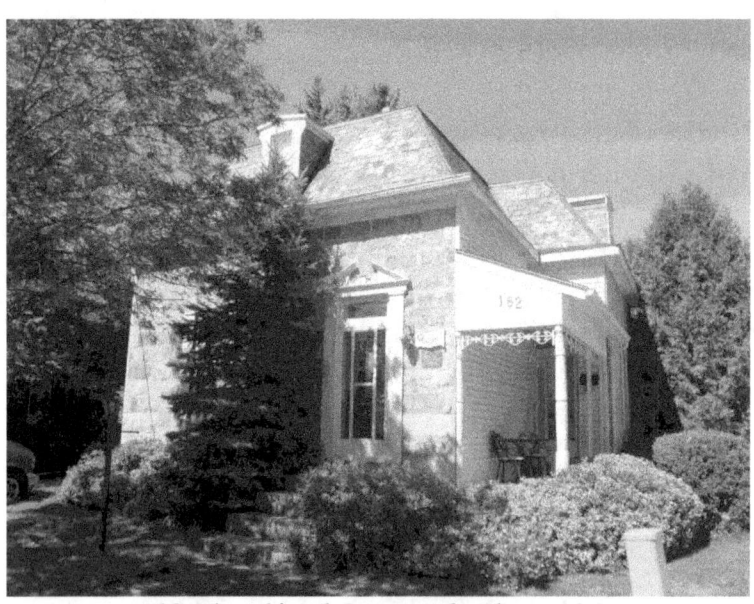

182 Blandford Street – built in 1867
first owner Charles Vincent
2 storey frame house with a stone front and a decorative roof

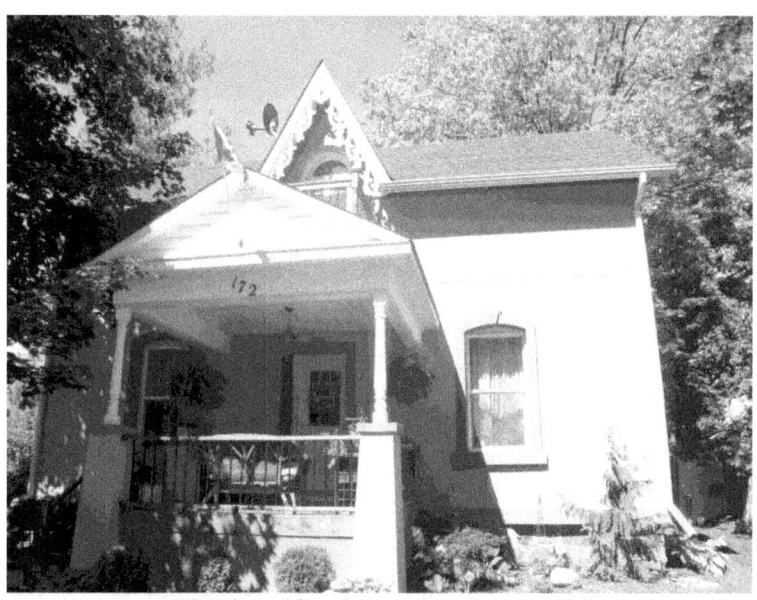

172 Blandford Street – built 1855
2 storey home with stone foundation, gingerbread trim on the centre gable, a porch on each floor
The present owners welcomed us, showed their home and shared a picnic lunch with us in their backyard.

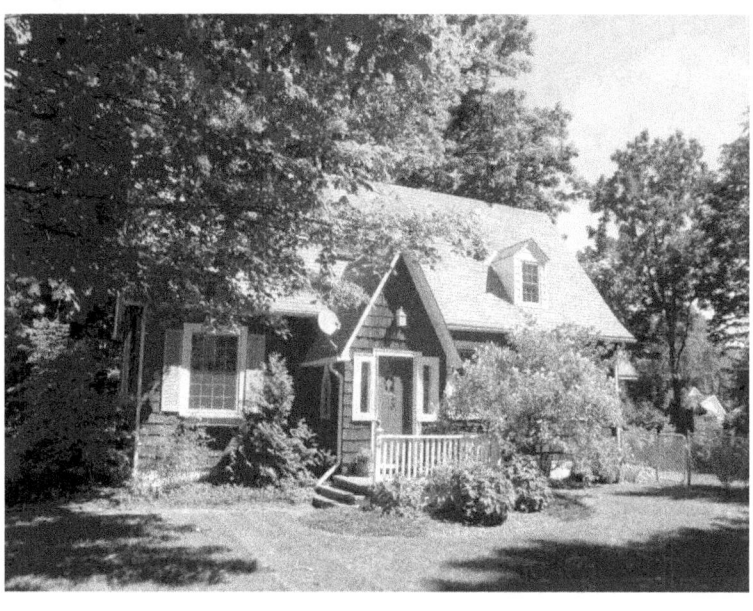

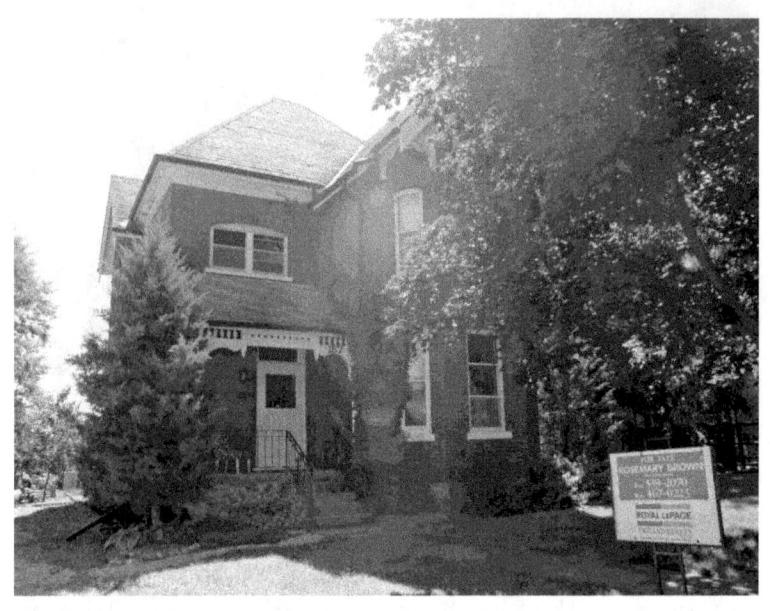

157 Blandford Street

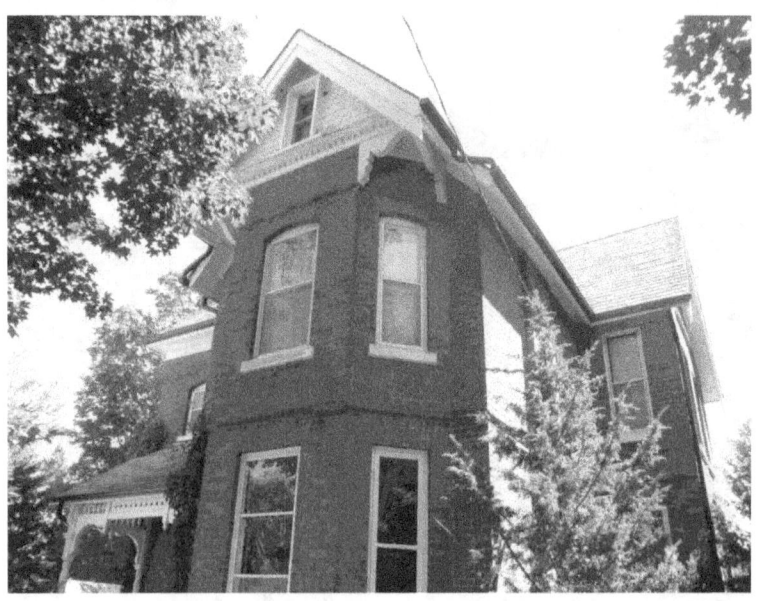

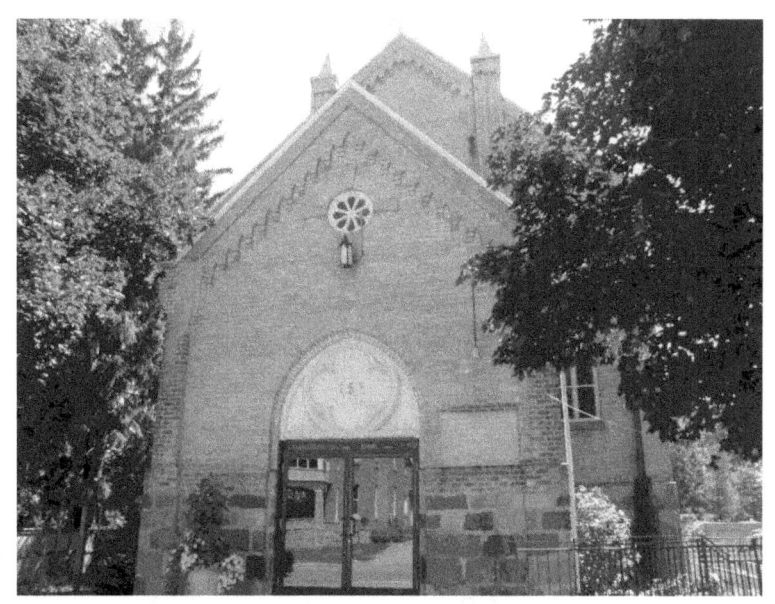

153 Blandford Street – old church

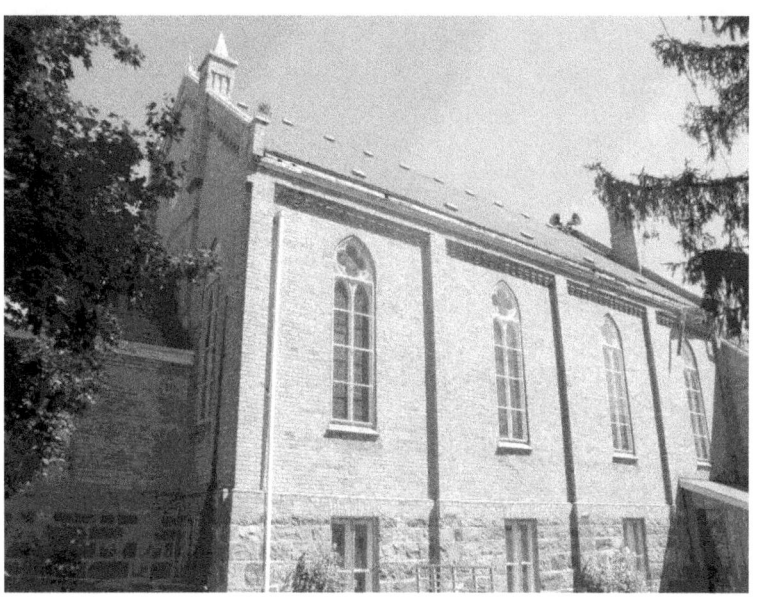

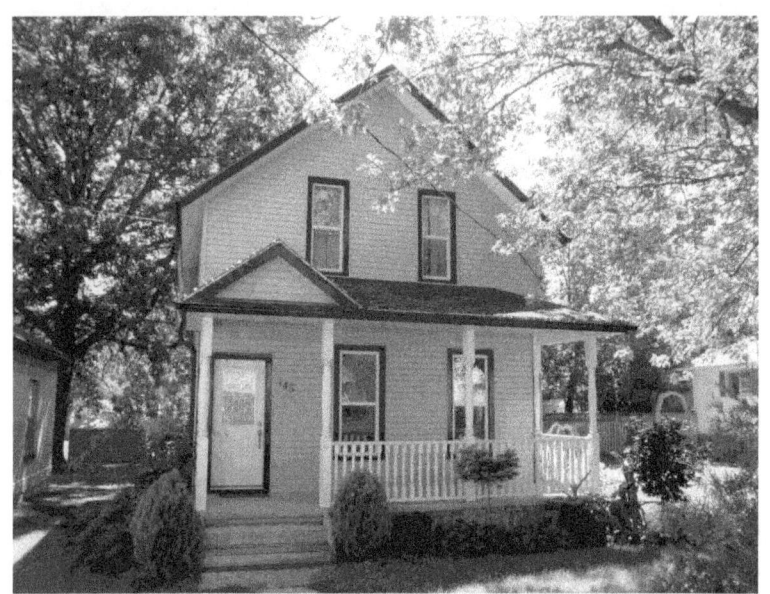

145 Blandford Street

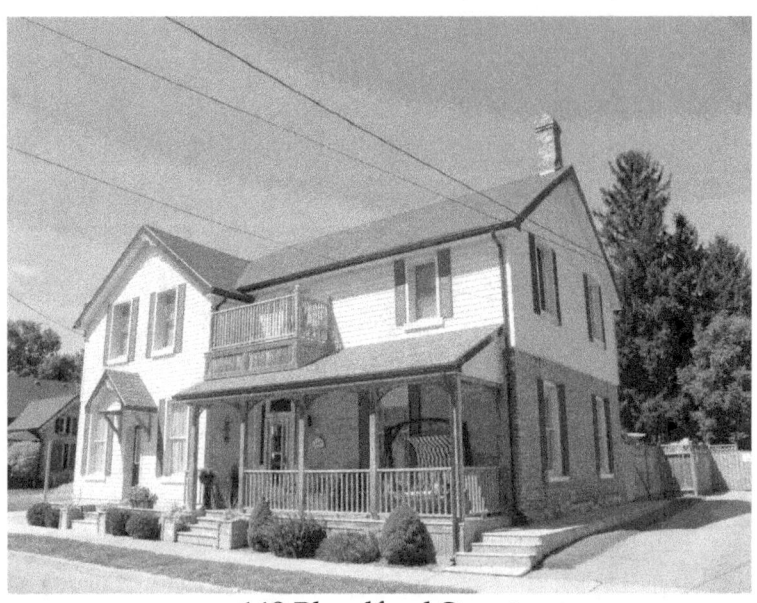

140 Blandford Street

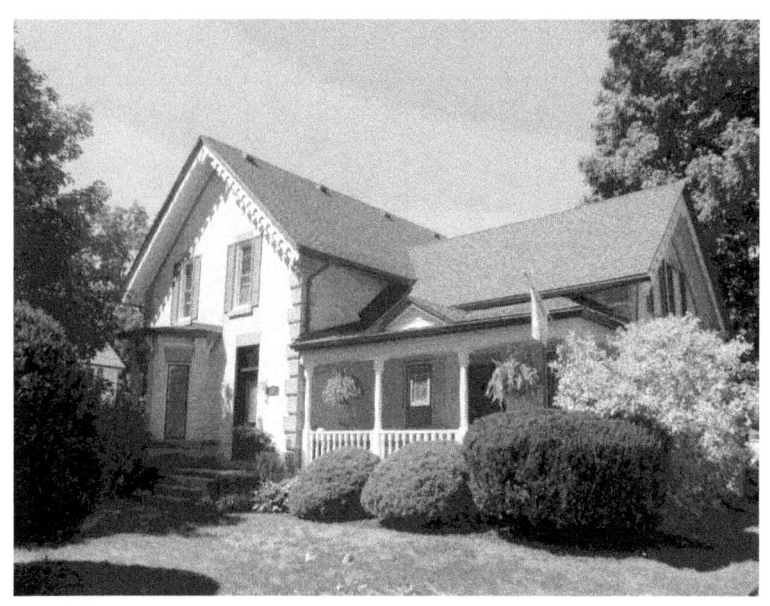

134 Blandford Street – built 1880
2 storey yellow brick with red brick corners and red brick
above windows, gingerbread trim

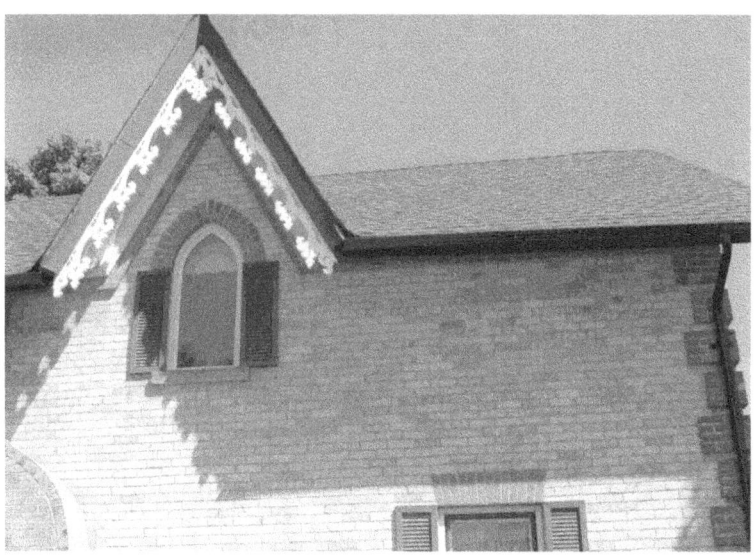

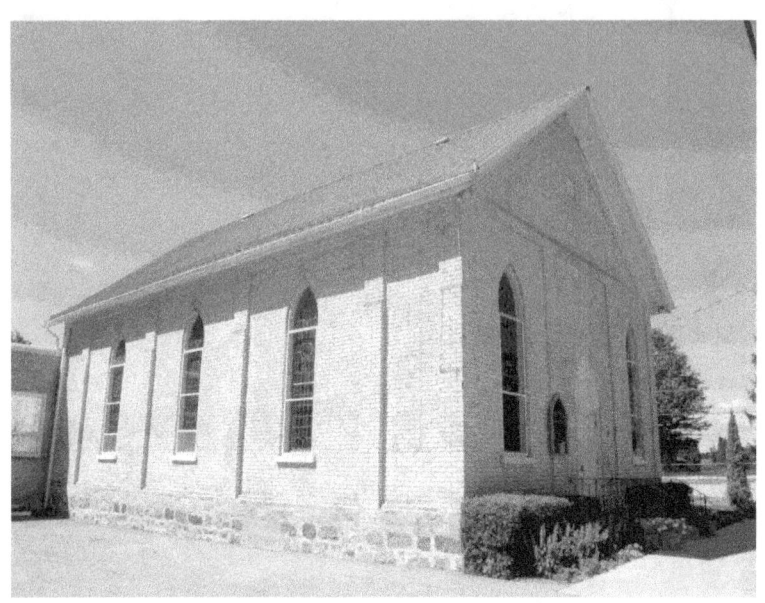

Methodist Church 1886
Now Innerkip United Church
11 Vincent Street

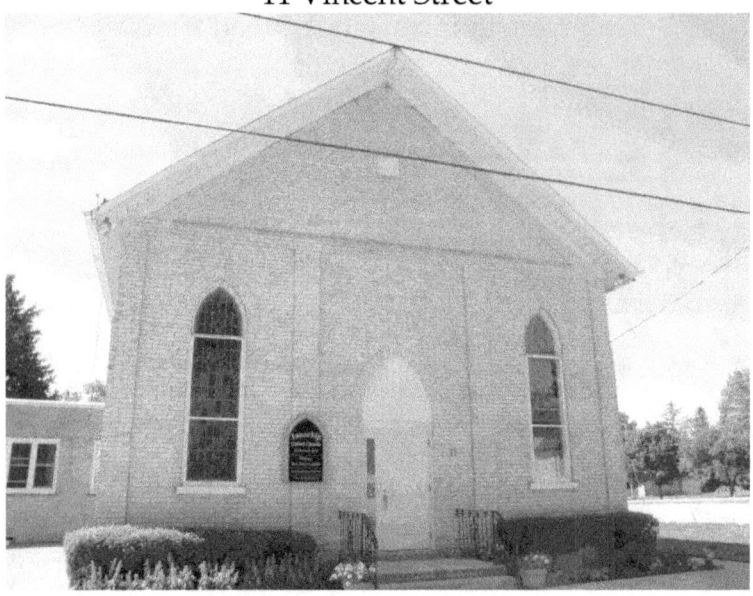

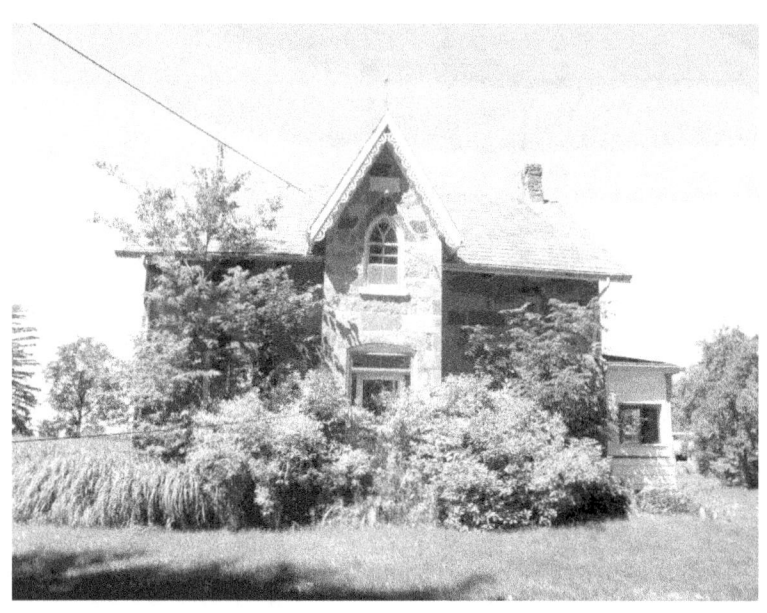

132 Coleman Street – built 1888
2 storey stone building, steel roof

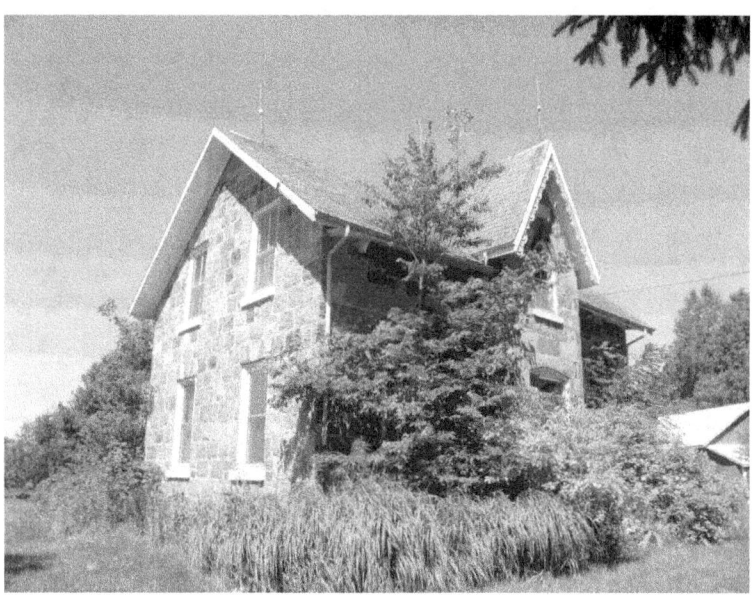

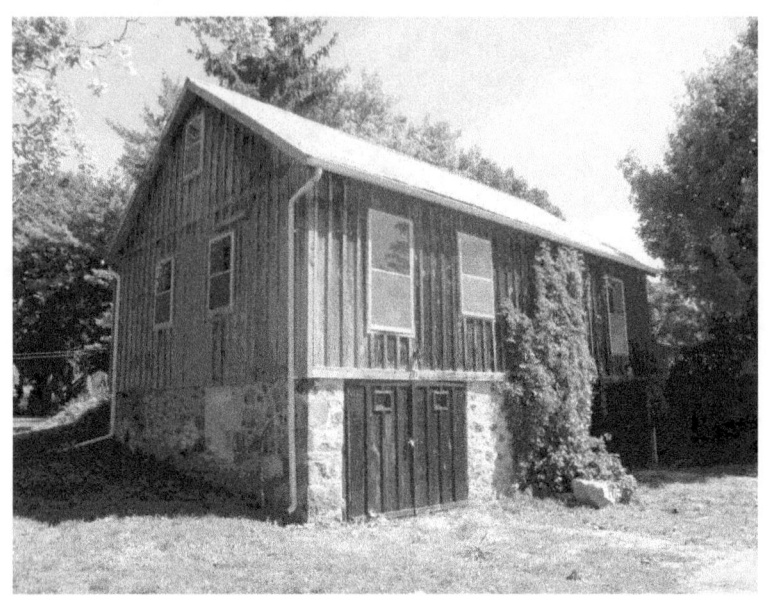

Barn with stone foundation

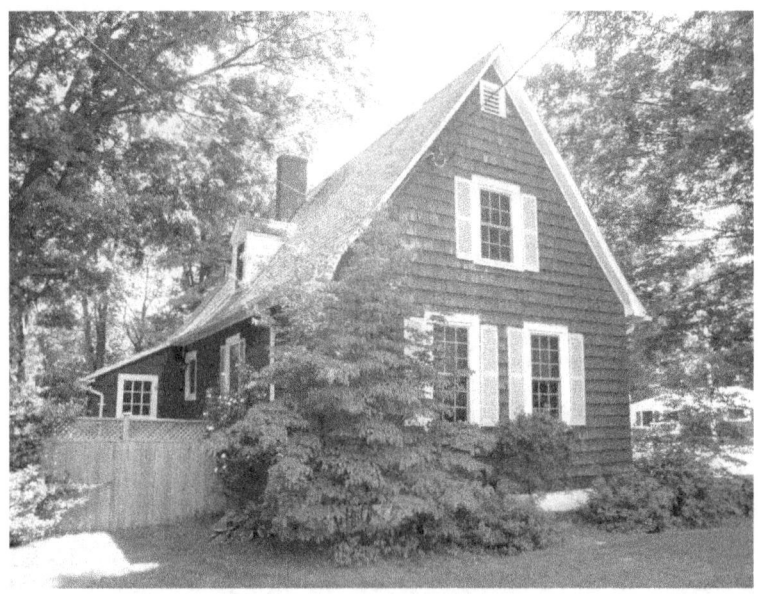

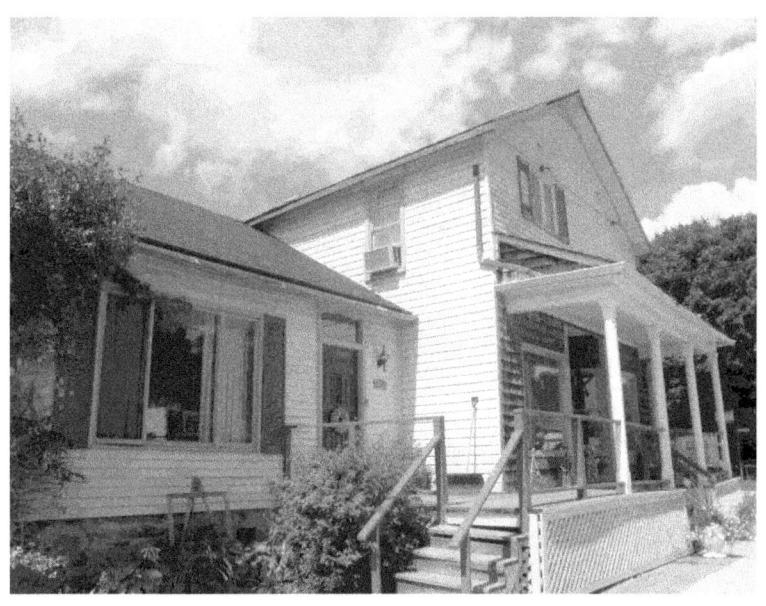

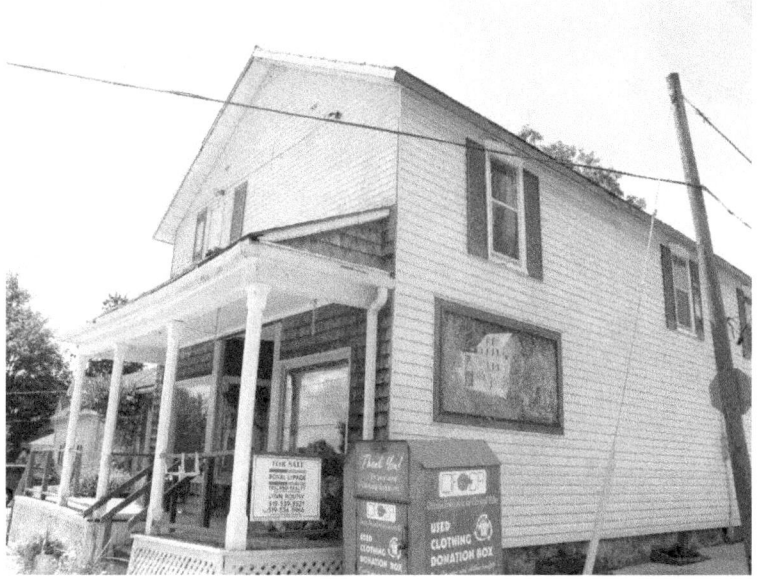

Mural of the old mill on the side of the building

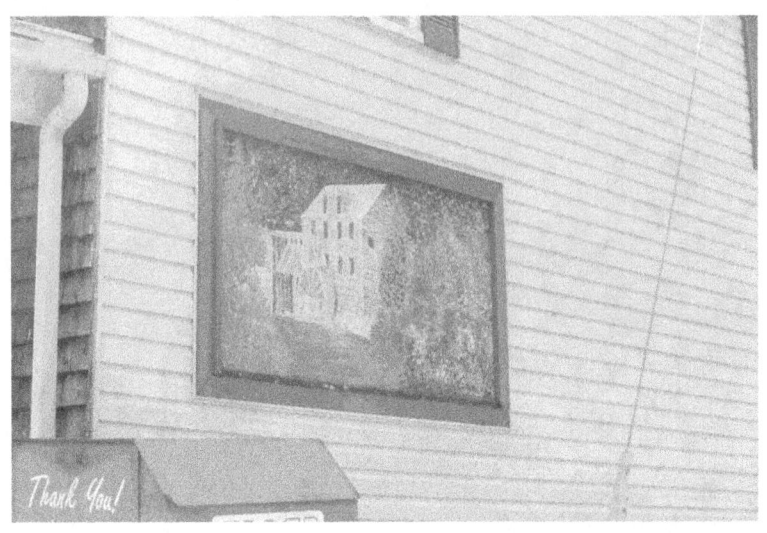

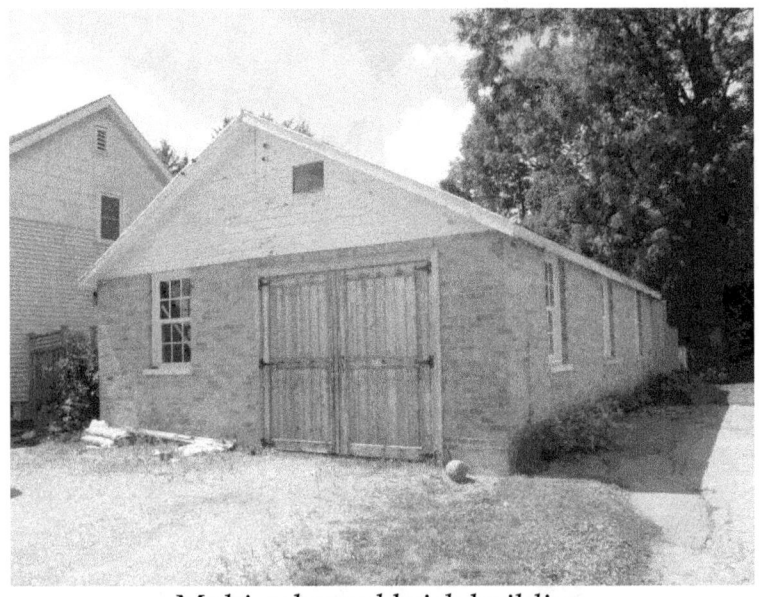

Multi-coloured brick building

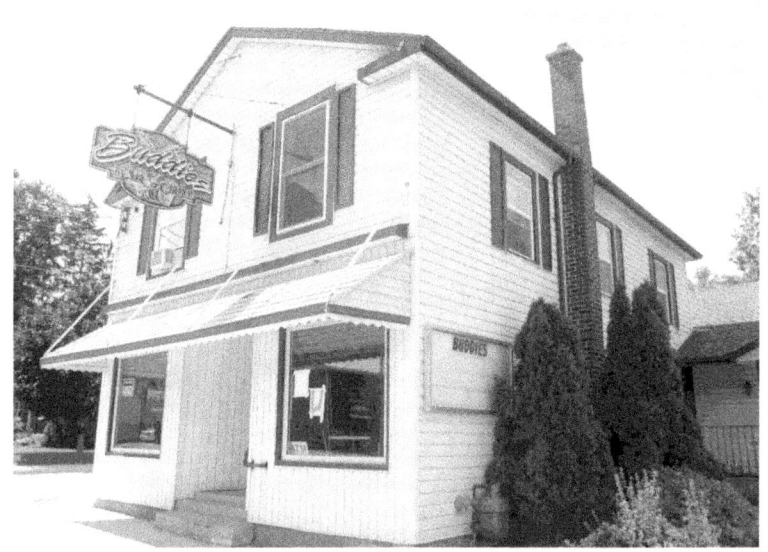

Buddies

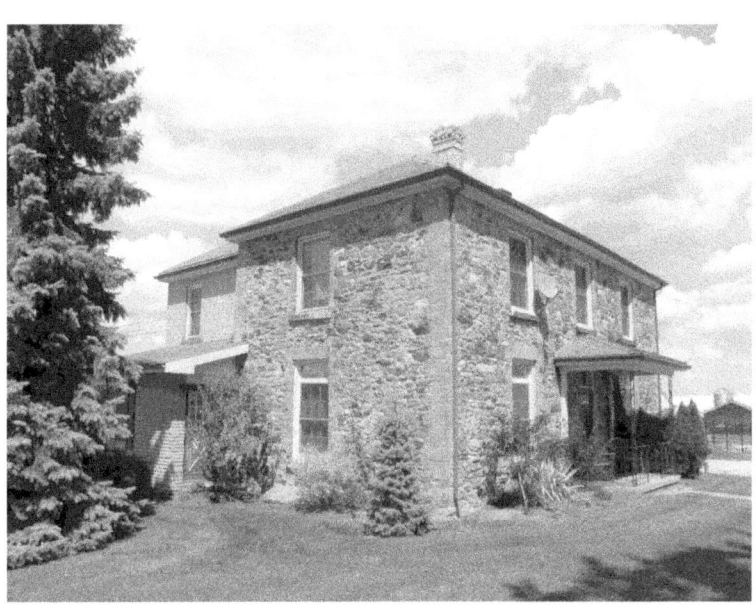

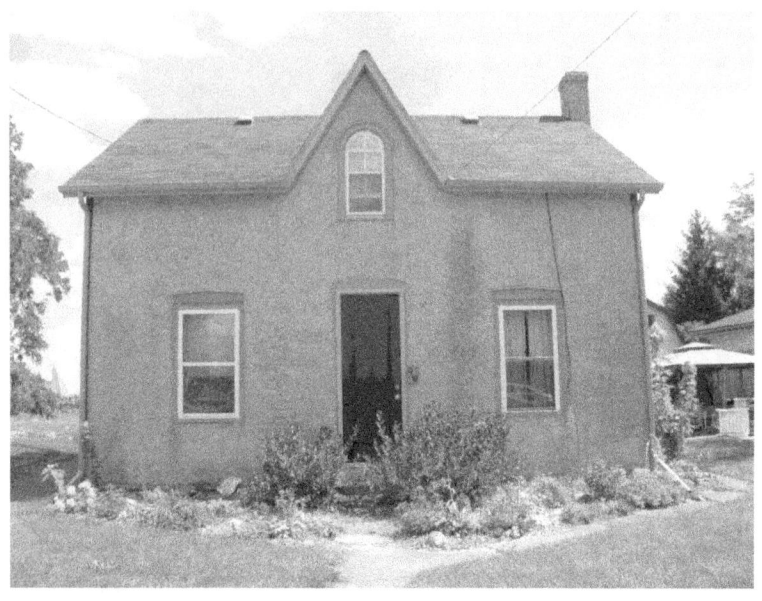

#99 - Gothic Revival style with centre gable

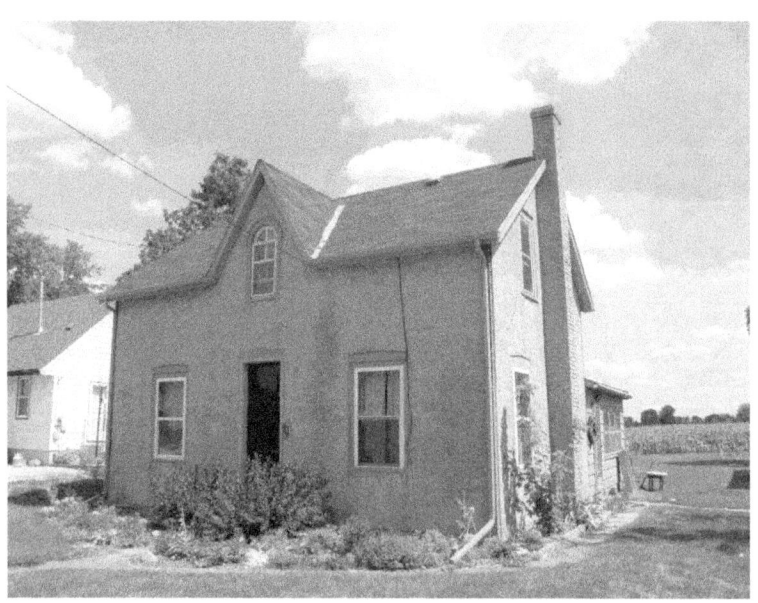

Woodstock

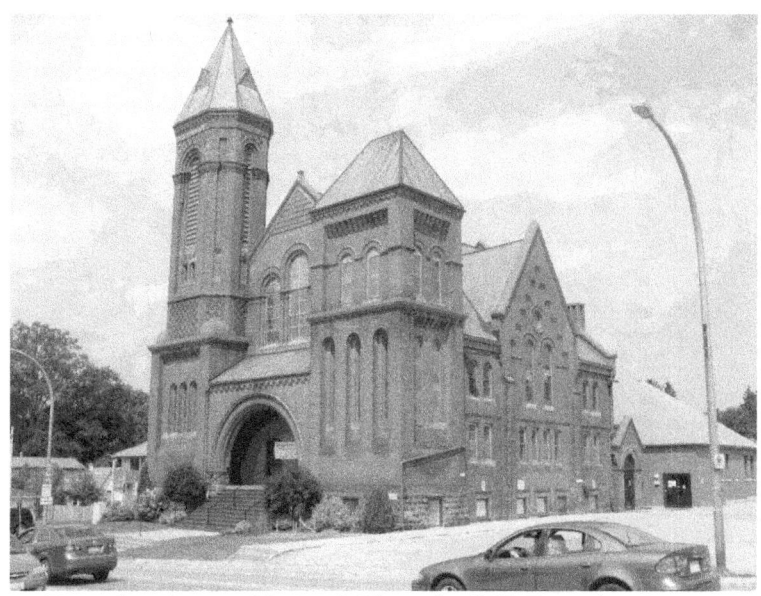

Dundas Street United Church, 285 Dundas Street
Built in 1889 of red brick and an artistically designed slate roof

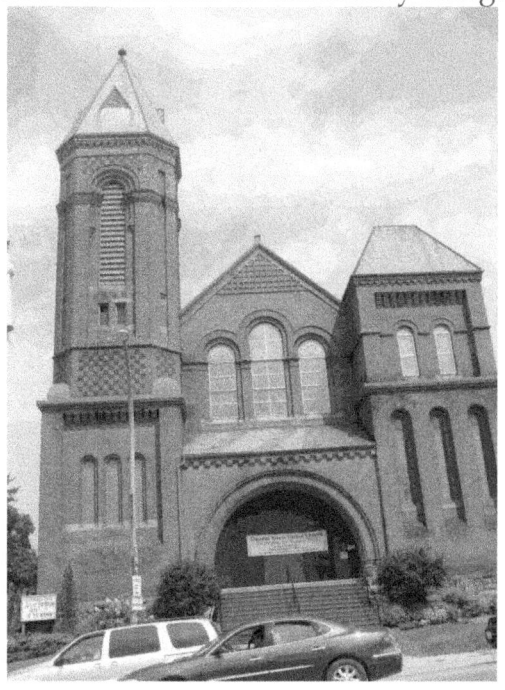

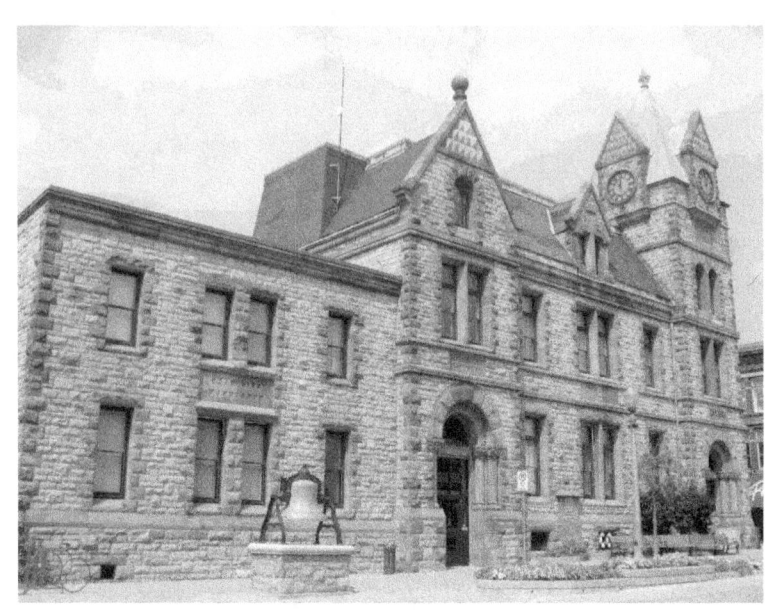

City Hall – built in 1899

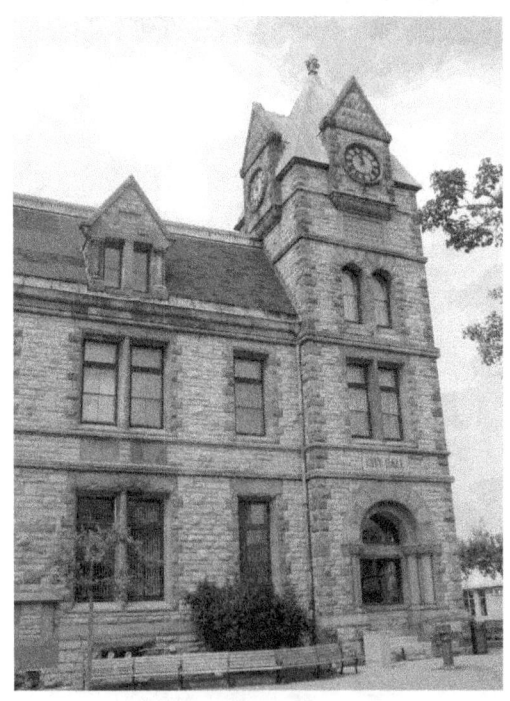

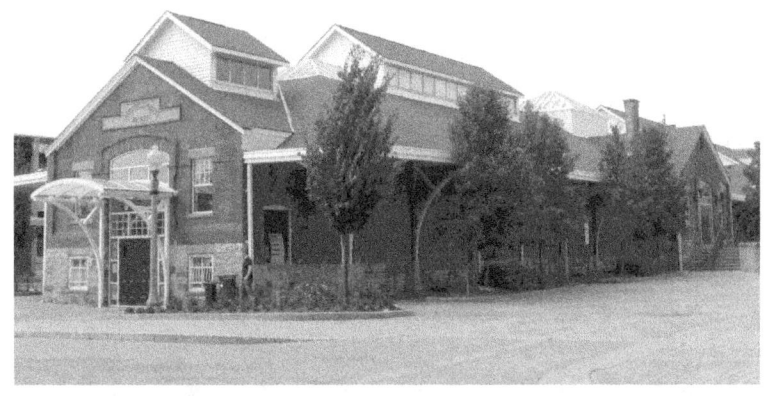

Woodstock Market – A.D. 1895

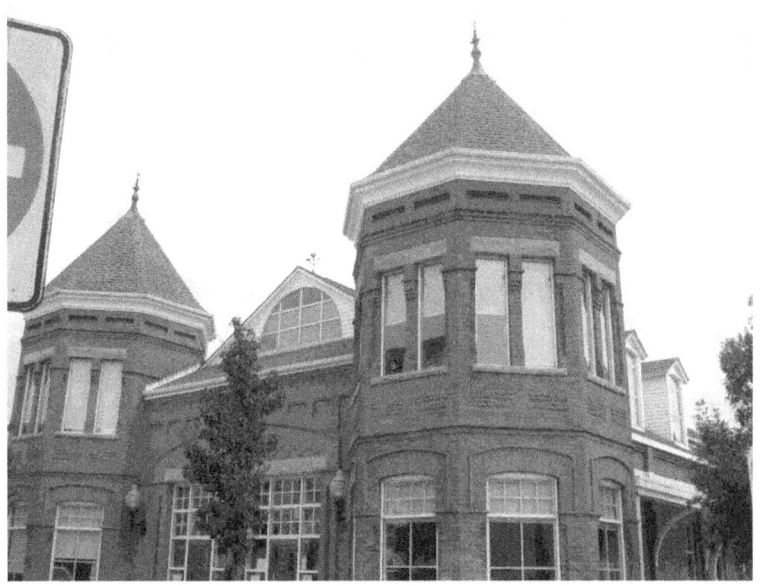

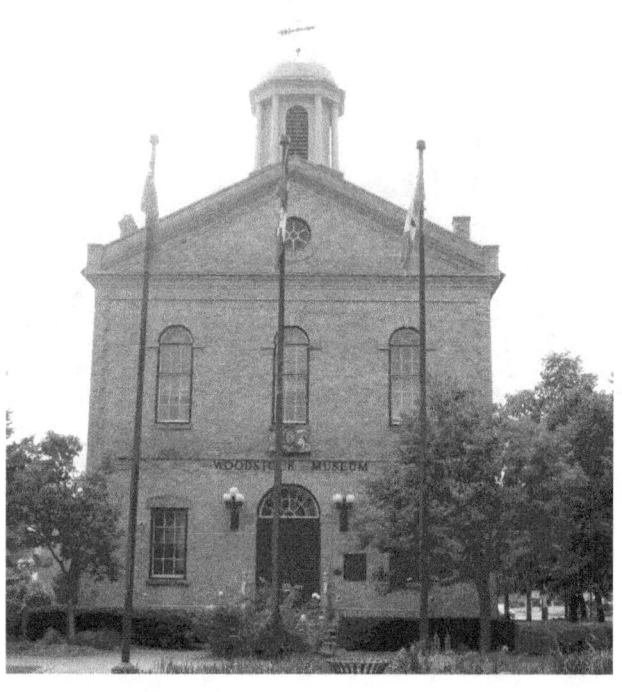

The Old Town Hall, constructed in 1851-52, was the centre of the municipal and social life of Woodstock, housing the local government, and serving as lecture hall, opera house and assize court. Although its lines are basically eighteenth century Palladian, exterior details such as round-headed windows with heavy surrounds reflect contemporary Italianate Revival influences. It currently houses the Woodstock Museum.

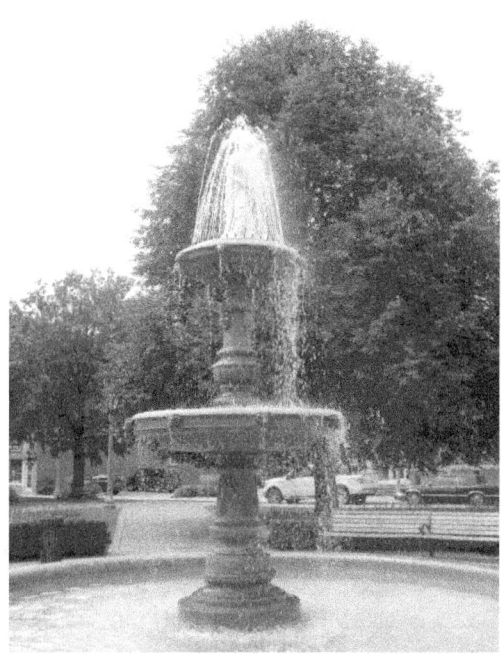

Pattulo's Fountain, located in front of the Old Town Hall, was erected in 1916 in honour of Andrew Pattulo, the head of the Sentinel Review at the time

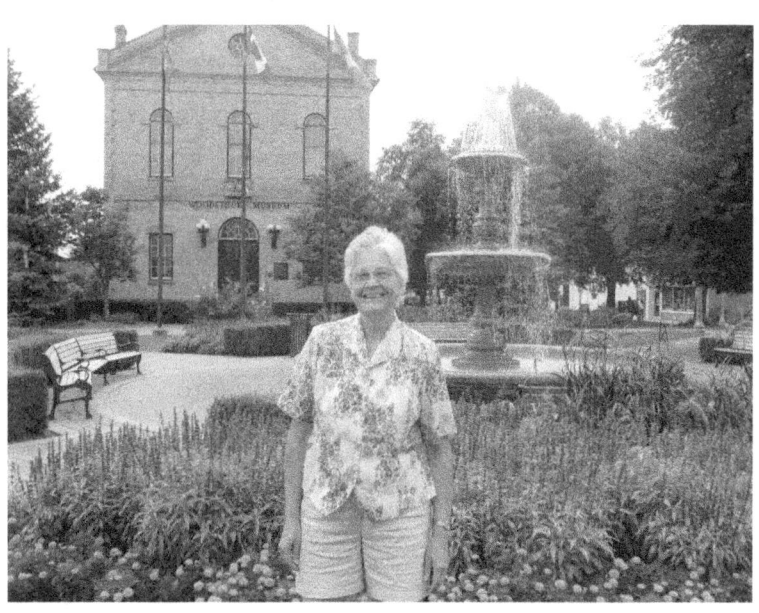

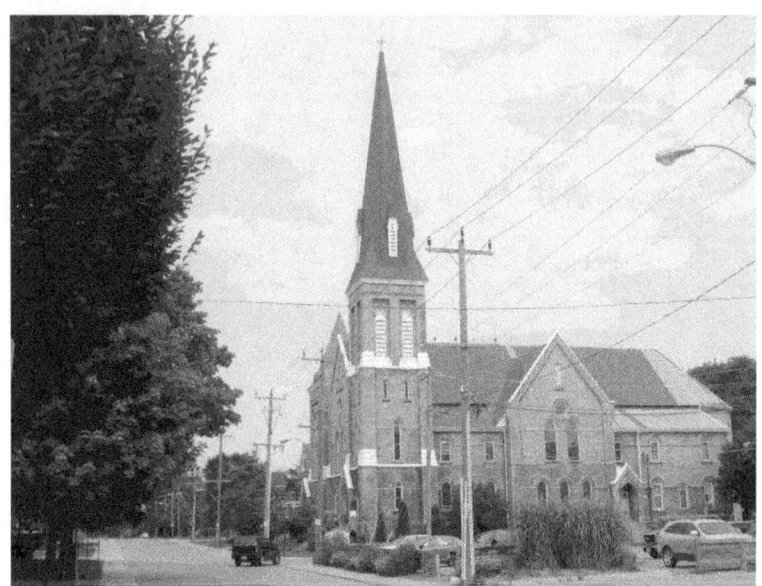

Faith United Church 34 Riddell Street, at the corner of
Adelaide Street – built in 1876

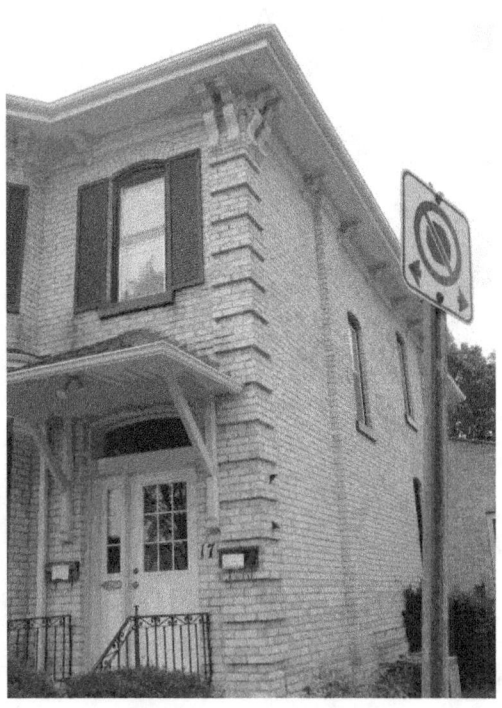

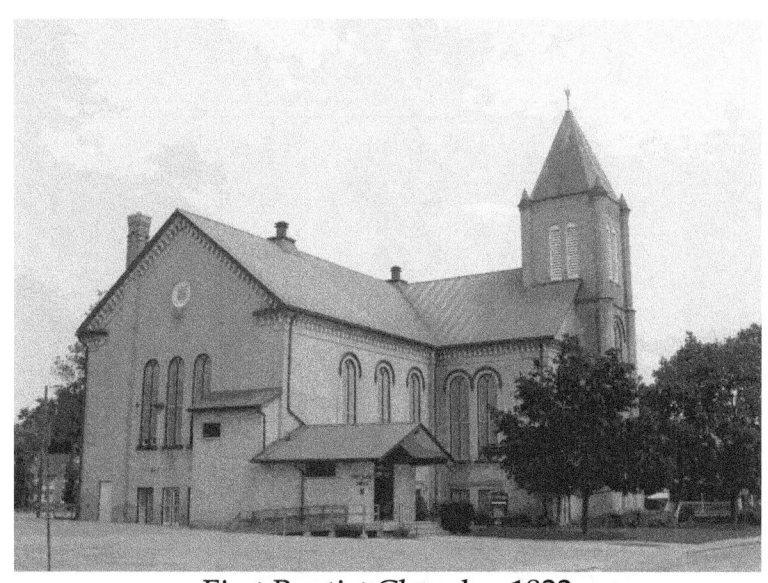

First Baptist Church – 1822
603 Adelaide Street
The ministry of the church began in 1822 and the people
celebrated their 175th anniversary in 1997.

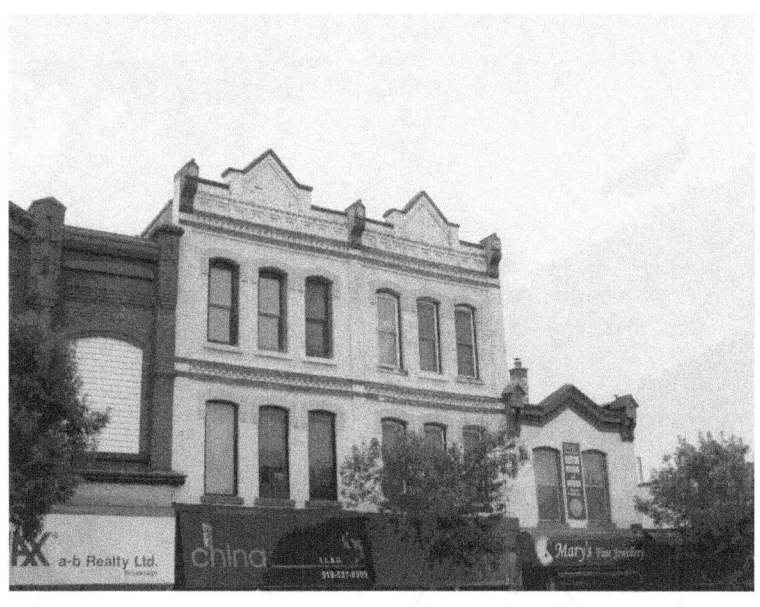

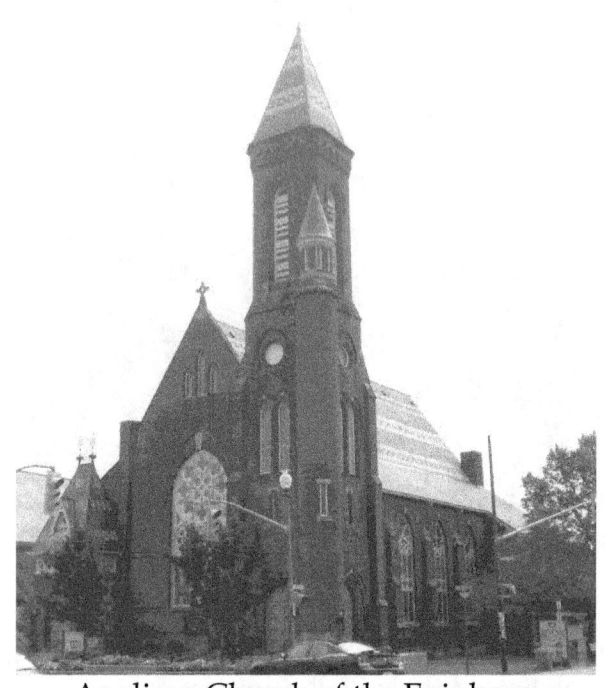

Anglican Church of the Epiphany
560 Dundas Street

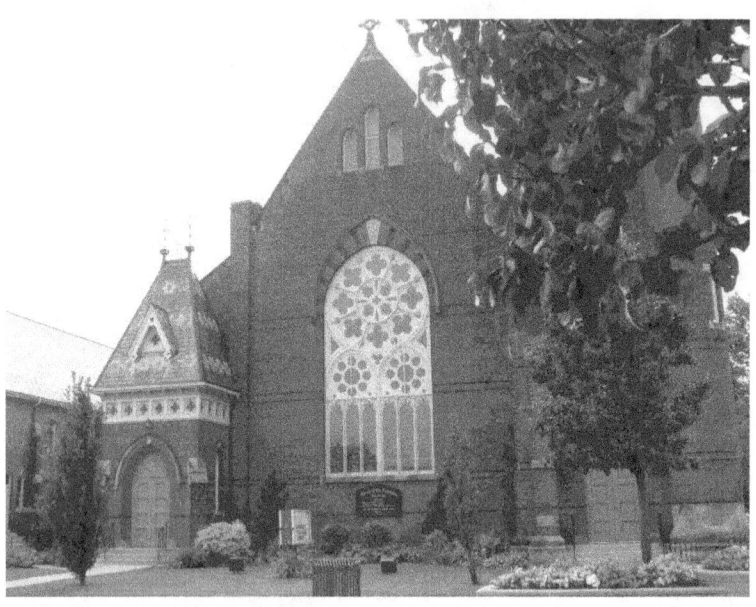

Huntingford

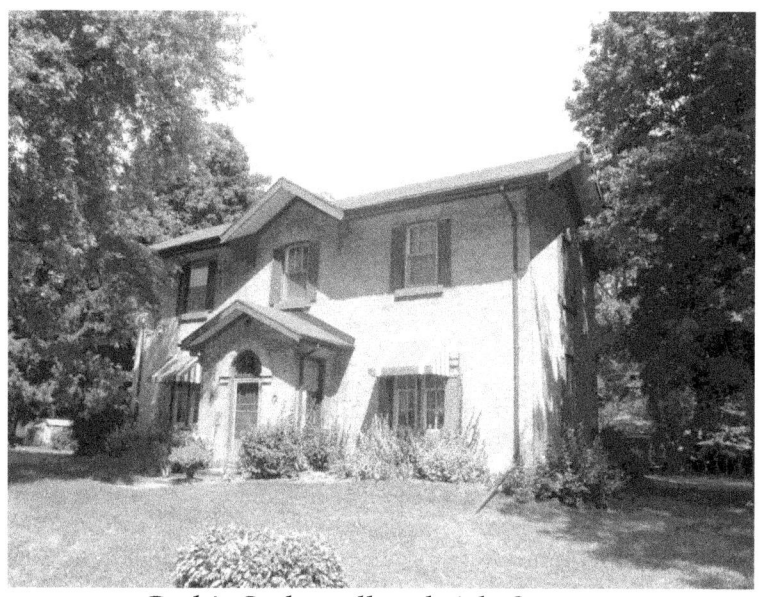

Gothic Style, yellow brick, 2 storey

Punkydoodles Corners

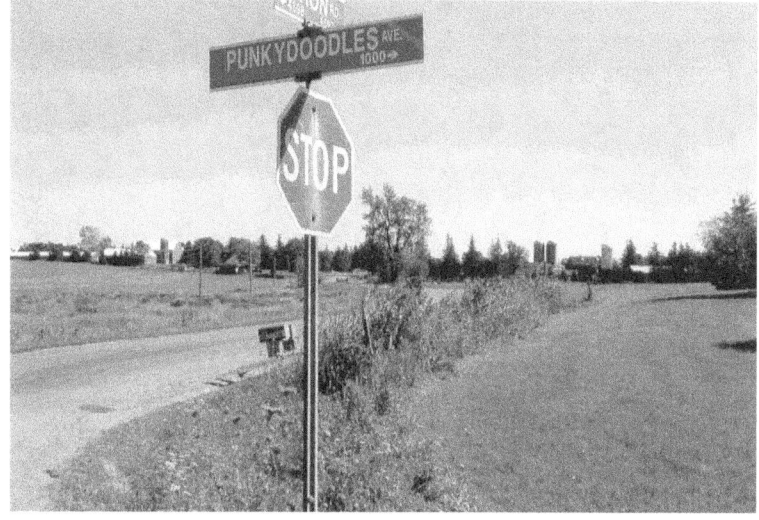

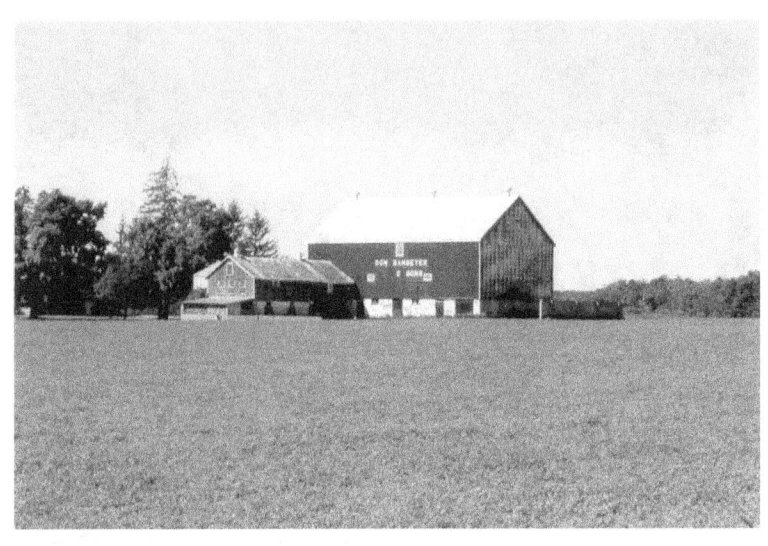

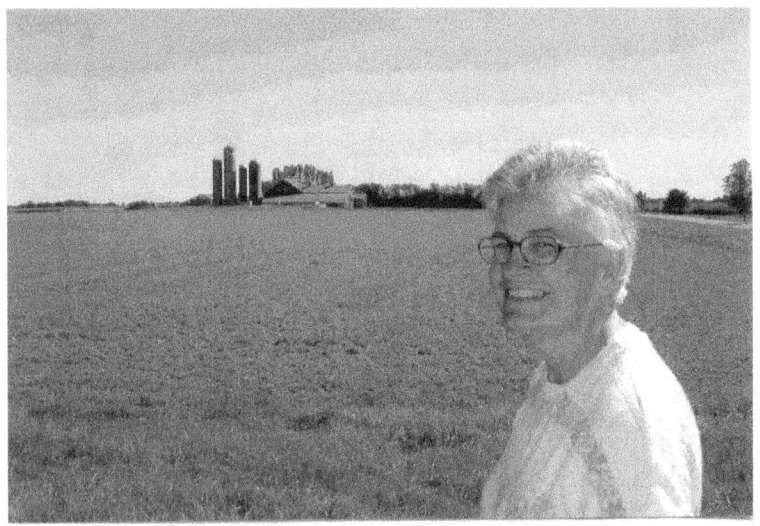

Hickson

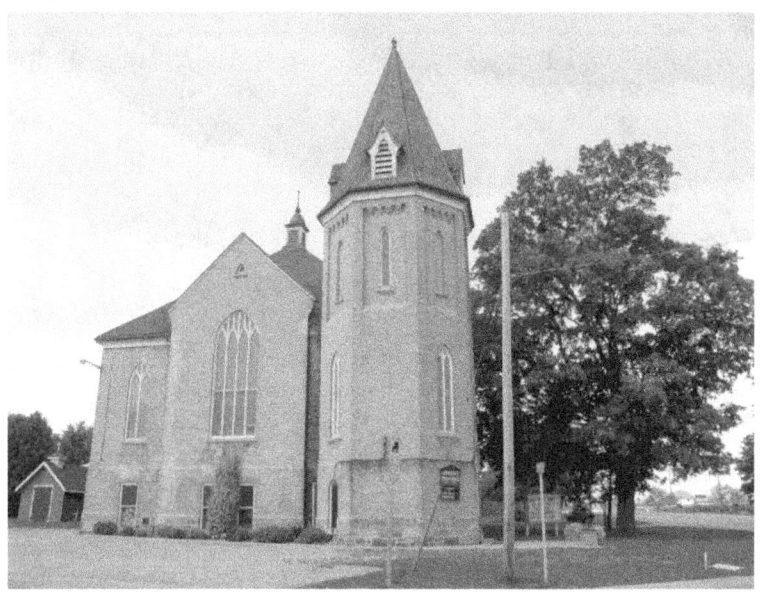

Hickson United Church opened in 1902 as a Wesleyan Methodist Church and joined the United Church in 1925.

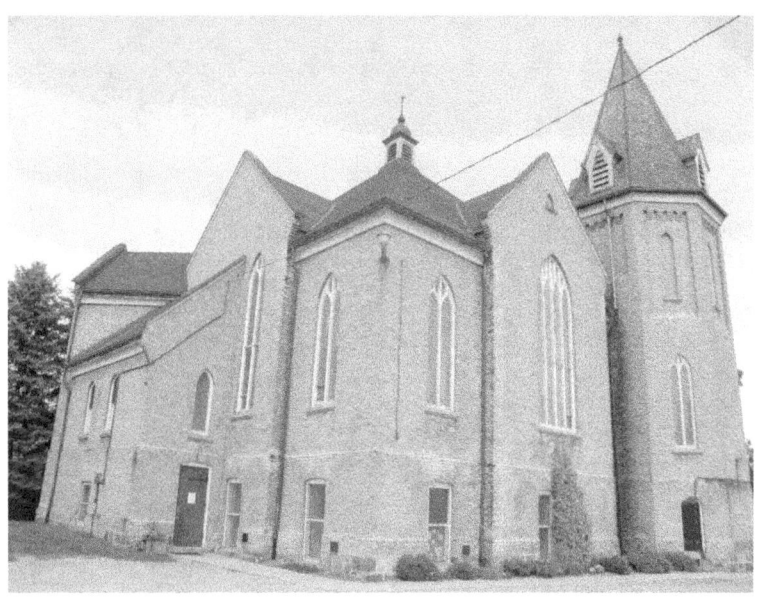

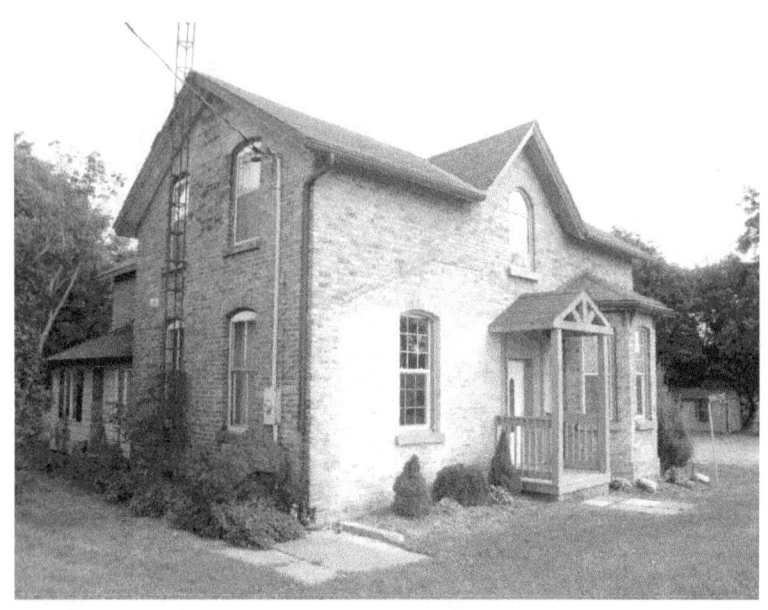

Multi-coloured brick home – Gothic Revival style

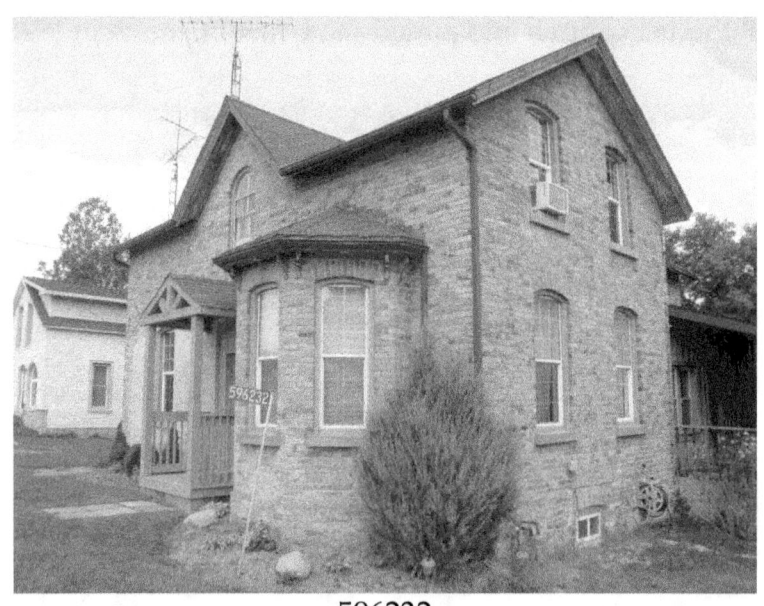

596232

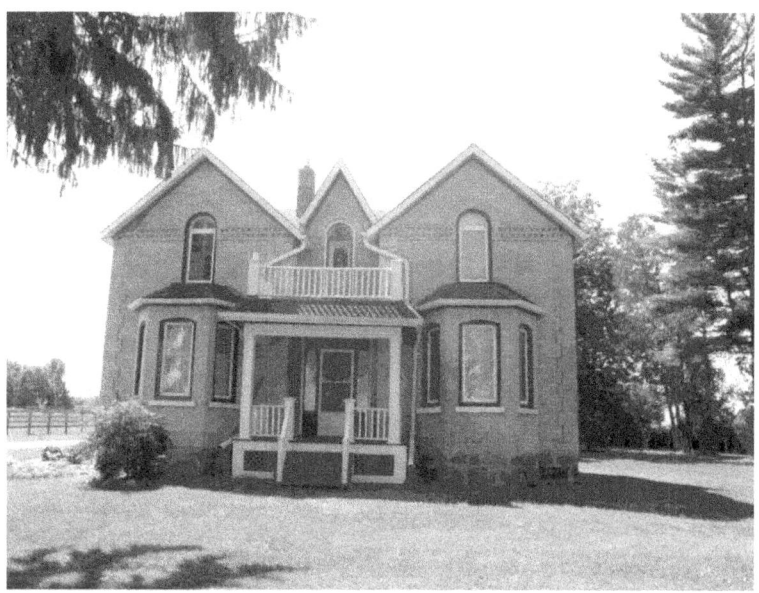

Victorian style, 2 storey, bay windows on lower level
Yellow brick

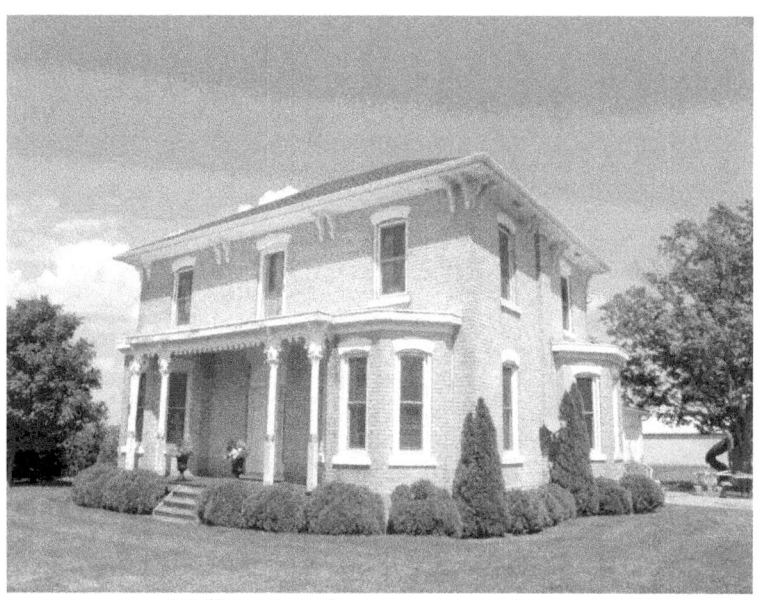

Yellow brick, two storey home
with bay windows on each corner
Note the paired cornice brackets under the eaves